Disney

Quotes

to Live

your

life by

First published in the UK in 2020 by Studio Press Books,
an imprint of Bonnier Books UK,
The Plaza, 535 King's Road, London, SW10 0SZ

studiopressbooks.co.uk
bonnierbooks.co.uk

Printed in China
2 4 6 8 10 9 7 5 3 1

All rights reserved
ISBN 978-1-78741-702-1

Designed by Nia Williams and Paul Calver
Cover designed by Nia Williams

DISNEY

Quotes to Live your life by

STUDIO PRESS

· Ariel ·

The Little Mermaid

Who says my dreams have to stay just dreams?

· Mike ·

Monsters, Inc.

You and i are a team. There is nothing more IMPORTANT than our FRIENDSHIP

· Grand Pabbie ·

Frozen II

All ONE can do is the next RIGHT THING

· Dory ·

Finding Nemo

WHEN
I LOOK
at YOU
I can FEEL it.
And I LOOK
at you,
and HOME
I'M

· Tiana ·

The Princess and the Frog

· Mr Incredible ·

The Incredibles

YOU are my GREATEST adventure

· Buzz Lightyear ·

Toy Story

· The Fairy Godmother ·

Cinderella

Even miracles take a little time

· Jasmine ·

Aladdin

· Merida ·

Brave

Our FATE lives within US YOU only have to be BRAVE enough to SEE it

· Tramp ·

Lady and the Tramp

There's a GREAT BIG hunk of world down there with NO fence around it

· Olaf ·

Frozen

· Edna Mode ·

The Incredibles

I never look back, DARLING. It DISTRACTS from the NOW

· Tiana ·

The Princess and the Frog

the only way to get what you want in this WORLD is THROUGH hard WORK

· Lumiere ·

Beauty and the Beast

You don't have *time* to be *timid* you must be **BOLD** and **DARING**

· Anton Ego ·

Ratatouille

Not Everyone can become a GREAT ARTIST, but a GREAT ARTIST can come from anywhere

· Narrator ·

Beauty and the Beast

BEAUTY
is
found
within

· Moana ·

Moana

SOMETIMES our STRENGTHS lie BENEATH the SURFACE

· Ernesto De La Cruz ·

Coco

SUCCESS
DOESN'T COME FOR FREE,
MIGUEL,
YOU HAVE TO DO
WHATEVER IT TAKES TO
SEIZE YOUR
MOMENT

· Sebastian ·

The Little Mermaid

· Baymax ·

Big Hero 6

It is
all
right to
CRY

· The Emperor ·

Mulan

The flower that blooms in adversity is the most RARE and Beautiful of all

· Timothy Q. Mouse ·

Dumbo

The very
things that held you
DOWN
are
Going to carry you
UP UP
UP UP and
and

· Anna ·

Frozen II

You are not responsible for their choices

· Grandmother Willow ·

Pocahontas

· Megara ·

Hercules

I'm a damsel, I'm in distress. I CAN HANDLE this

· Judy ·

Zootopia

The more
we try to
UNDERSTAND
one another,
The more
EXCEPTIONAL
each of us
will be

· Snow White ·

Snow White and the Seven Dwarfs

REMEMBER

you're the

ONE

who can fill the

world

with

sunshine

· Thumper ·

Bambi

· Mufasa ·

The Lion King

EVERYTHING you SEE exists TOGETHER in a delicate BALANCE

· Mama Imelda ·

Coco

· Big Mama ·

The Fox and the Hound

FOREVER is a long, long time, and TIME has a way of changing things

· Rapunzel ·

Tangled

Venture outside your comfort zone. The rewards are worth it

· Ralph ·

Wreck-It Ralph

There's NO ONE I'd RATHER be THAN ME

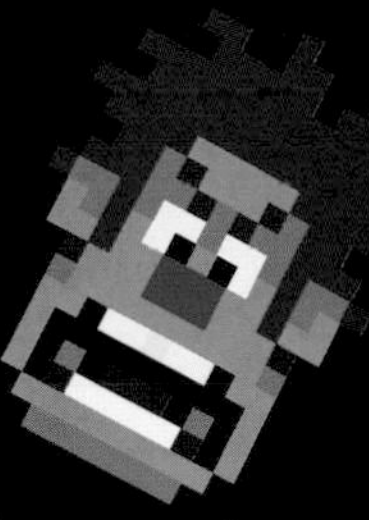

· Mushu ·

Mulan

We Started this thing Together, and that's how we'll finish it

· Mrs Potts ·

Beauty and the Beast

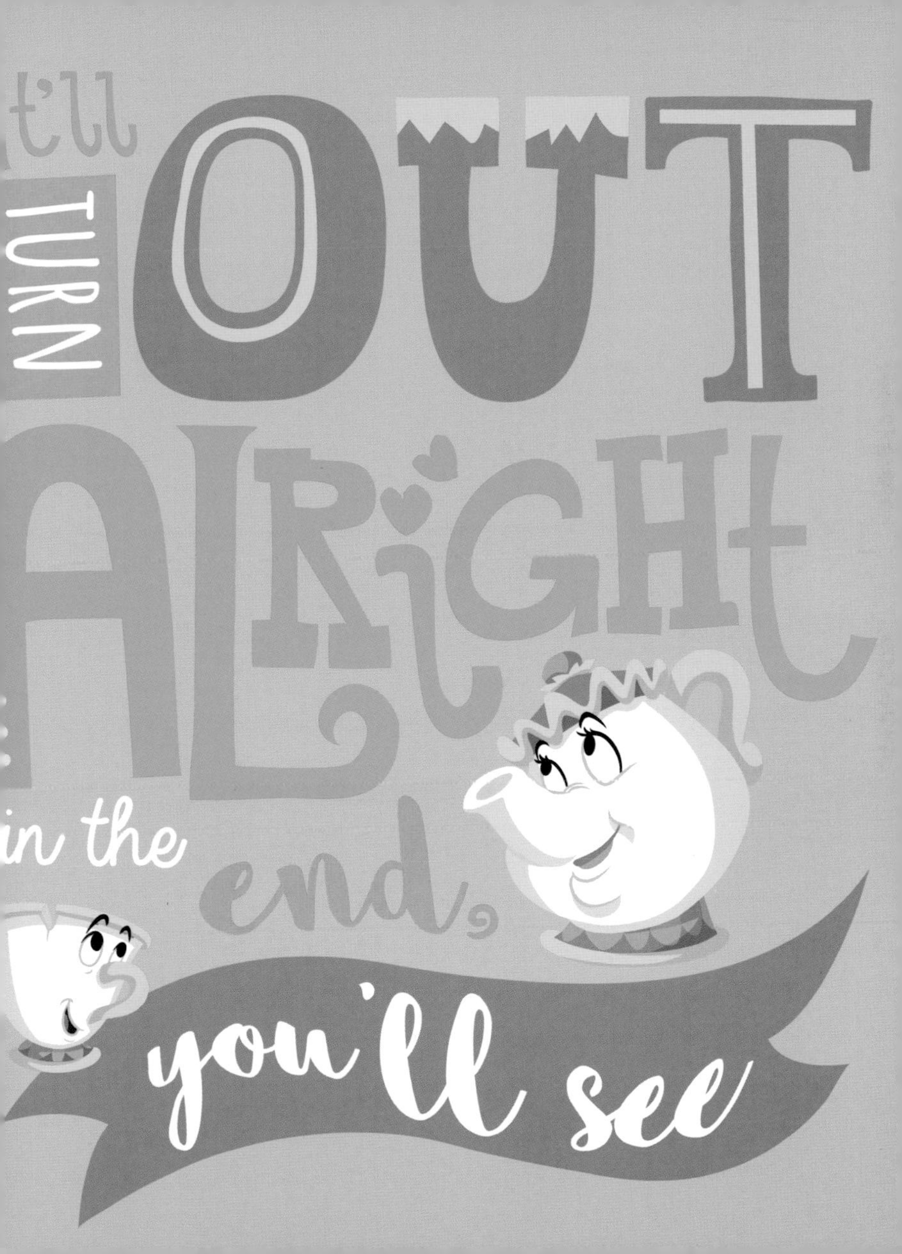
t'll
TURN
OUT
ALRiGHT
in the
end,
you'll see

· Grimsby ·

The Little Mermaid

FAR BETTER
than **ANY**
DREAM
GIRL is **ONE**
of FLESH and
BLOOD

· Belle ·

Beauty and the Beast

We're
together
now.
EVERYTHING'S
going
to be
fine...

· Rafiki ·

The Lion King

Oh yes, the past can hurt. But the way I see it, you can either run from it... or Learn from it

· Pocahontas ·

Pocahontas

THIS
is the
PATH
I CHOOSE

· The Blue Fairy ·

Pinocchio

Always let YOUR conscience be YOUR guide

· Denahi ·

Brother Bear

Small things
BECOME
Winter TURNS
to *spring*
thing
always
CHANGES
into another

BIG

ONE

· Alice ·

Alice in Wonderland

But that's just the trouble with me. I give myself very good advice, but I seldom follow it

· Elastigirl ·

The Incredibles

· Cinderella ·

Cinderella

They CAN'T ORDER me to STOP dreaming

· Remy ·

Ratatouille

THE
ONLY THING
PREDICTABLE
ABOUT LIFE
IS ITS
UNPREDICTABILITY

· Mulan ·

Mulan

Maybe what I really wanted was to prove I could do things right

· Gramma Tala ·

Moana

There is nowhere you could go that I won't be with you

· Phil ·

Hercules

GIVING UP is for ROOKIES

· Aurora ·

Sleeping Beauty

· Cogsworth ·

Beauty and the Beast

if it's NOT BAROQUE, Don't FIX it

· The Genie ·

Aladdin

REMEMBER, BEE YOURSELF

· Woody ·

Toy Story 2

I can't stop Andy from growing up. But I wouldn't miss it for the world

· Jenny ·

Finding Dory

You can do **whatever** you put your **mind** to